under
SAIL

Published by Artisan

A Division of Workman Publishing, Inc.

708 Broadway

New York, New York 10003

www.workman.com

First Published in the UK by Scriptum Editions

Created by Co & Bear Productions (UK) Ltd.

Copyright © 2000 Co & Bear Productions (UK) Ltd.

Photographs copyright © 1999 Simon McBride.

Additional images copyright, see picture credits.

Library of Congress Cataloging-in-Publication

Glenn, David

    Under sail : Aboard the world's finest boats /

    written by David Glenn ; Photographed by Simon

    McBride.—1st ed.

        p. cm.

    ISBN 1-57965-171-2

    1. Yachts—Pictorial works. 2. Yachting—Pictorial works.

    I. Title.

    VM331.G58 2000

    623.8'2023—dc21

                                00–059429

Printed and bound in Italy at Officine Grafiche De Agostini.

Color reproduction by Bright Arts Graphics, Singapore.

First edition

10 9 8 7 6 5 4 3 2 1

under SAIL

ABOARD THE WORLD'S FINEST BOATS

written by DAVID GLENN
photographed by SIMON McBRIDE

ARTISAN | NEW YORK

Contents

Introduction

A century ago, anyone building a private yacht must have thought it inconceivable that the very same vessel could be afloat, in commission and competitive a century later. While only a handful of yachts in this book were built that long ago, there is every reason to suggest that many will see in the 22nd century, such is the power of their appeal and the ability of modern technology to keep them 'alive'. Yachts like *Tuiga* and *Orion* may have been built close to the turn of the 19th century but they are probably more active now than they have ever been. In a relatively short period in history, yachting has come full circle.

A fascination for the style of a bygone era and perhaps the absence of character in modern materials have led to a resurgence of interest in classic yachts. Wood, especially the short-grained, hardwood varieties, has a warmth, texture and appearance that no modern material can emulate. And when the work of 19th-century naval architects is examined, no present day scientist could fail to be impressed by their ingenuity. The gaff rig itself, complex yet remarkably efficient, is an example. The current fascination for such seemingly archaic ways of going sailing is based on intrigue – how did people solve problems a century ago? – and a desire to see those formulae applied to the way we go sailing today.

Although yachting did not become a popular pastime of any significance until the mid to late 19th century, those yachts that did exist, at least on the racing circuit, were large and splendid. Captains of industry were attracted by the glamour attached to a sport in which the Prince

of Wales was a regular participant aboard *Britannia*. Royal patronage attracted names like Sopwith and Lipton on one side of the Atlantic and Vanderbilt, Lawrence and Astor on the other. The German Kaiser was a keen Big Class yachtsman, and the Spanish and Scandinavian royal families were, and still are, very much at the forefront of competition.

Perhaps there is something in the glamour of yesteryear that has seen a growing determination among present-day yacht owners – who might otherwise have bought a modern vessel – to preserve the past. Tom Perkins saved one of the finest yachts of the pre-war era, *Mariette* of 1915, driven by a fascination for authenticity and, as an American, the desire to save one of the best works of Nathanael Herreshoff, the celebrated American designer.

Mariette is proof of the appeal of traditional craftsmanship, and nowhere is this craft more apparent than in a yacht's accommodation. The superyacht of today can astound, such is the level of sophistication seen below decks, but it is perhaps nothing compared to standards set aboard the so-called 'salt water palaces' of the last century. Amid solid hardwood panelling, silk upholstery, crystal chandeliers, solid fuel fires and steam driven auxiliary systems, owners were not only able to enjoy the comforts of home, but were then able to call on a crew to secure everything prior to going racing.

The same is possible today, but instead of painstakingly preparing the accommodation for sea, it is removed entirely, packed into containers and forwarded to the yacht's next destination where it is reinstalled. Laminates and cappings now hide lightweight structures where once solid timber was the only option.

It is innovation like this that has inspired a resurgence in luxury yachting. The yacht has always been a status symbol for the wealthy, but now these vessels are not merely a measure of the owner's wealth; they provide an indication of what sort of person they may be. Power or sail, racing or cruising, modern or classical? The style can be telling. The demands of modern life have also made the yacht the perfect vessel for escape. Owners are able to find privacy aboard a yacht that no hotel or private house can offer. Access to some of the most remote places on earth is also theirs.

Momentous changes in communication and navigation have also made the yachting lifestyle more appealing and accessible than ever. At the turn of the century almost all communication was done by flag signalling which was extraordinarily sophisticated. For instance, there were simple flag sequences for inviting guests aboard including one specifically for 'May we borrow your first violinist?'.

Because private speech, data and images can now been sent via satellite from any ocean, anywhere in the world, owners feel much more willing to base themselves aboard for periods of time without feeling cut off. Not only can they hold their business meetings aboard, entertain the press when required and keep it at arm's length at other times, but they can also sail

OPPOSITE The magnificent J-Class yacht *Endeavour* was originally built for the aviator T.O.M. Sopwith to challenge for the America's Cup. This photograph shows her in her original form in the 1930s with a distinctive quadrilateral foresail set. In the 1980s she was fully restored by American Elizabeth Meyer.

freely wherever they want. Satellites have also transformed navigation. Navigators, once reliant on using a sextant, can now use the Global Positioning System, which pinpoints its user's position to within a metre anywhere on earth. The other dramatic breakthrough has come in the handling of large yachts. A century ago scores of men were required to sail yachts of 130ft or more, and indeed whole coastal communities in the UK and American eastern seaboard revolved around their menfolk being employed to crew gentlemen's yachts.

For the racing fraternity today there is little option but to employ a full crew, although large cruising yachts have dramatically reduced crew numbers in the past few years. 'Automation' and 'press-button' are the words which pepper yacht specifications today and owners can maintain a high degree of privacy by employing four or five crew aboard a 140-ft yacht. This has certainly had something to do with the popularity and return of the classic.

Whether classical or contemporary, designed for the race course or simply cruising the oceans of the world, large sailing yachts retain a mystique and beauty which can be mesmeric. But the essential appeal of sailing is perhaps derived as much from the aesthetics of its craft as from its basic use of natural energy. As Uffa Fox, possibly Britain's most celebrated yachtsman and designer, once said: 'Sailing has advantages over other sports. Once you have your vessel, you do not take anything from the earth's resources to enjoy your racing, cruising or day sailing. Your power is invisible and silent and there is always wind to spare.'

LEFT The celebrated designer and yacht builder Charles Nicholson at the helm of Herman Andreae's *Candida* during a Big Class race in the Solent off the Isle of Wight around 1930. The yacht immediately to leeward is the royal yacht *Britannia* with Sir Mortimer Singer's *Astra* following in her wake.

BELOW *Candida* under full sail including a vast balloon jib. Despite the enormous amount of sail area carried by these yachts, 30 to 40 crew would be shipped aboard to race in near gale force wind conditions.

Mariette
Gaff Schooner–138ft

Of all the yachts belonging to the modern era of rebuild and restoration, the Nathanael Herreshoff-designed 138-ft schooner *Mariette* is regarded as one of the most outstanding. Her reputation is built not only on the quality of her restoration, but also the way in which she is used – often and hard.

Considered to be one of the American designer's speediest and sleekest schooners when she was launched in 1915, *Mariette*'s performance is even more impressive today, thanks to modern equipment, advanced sail cloth and an owner who likes to push his yachts to the limit. Tom Perkins, a New York-born engineer and venture capitalist, races *Mariette* in a string of classic yacht regattas in the Mediterranean during the late summer and then crosses the Atlantic to do battle in events like Antigua Classic Week.

The schooner was built by the Herreshoff Manufacturing Company for Frederick J. Brown as a close sistership to Harold S. Vanderbilt's *Vagrant,* and until World War II she flourished under careful ownership. After being requisitioned by the US Coastguard, she began a long period of deterioration.

It was not until the 1980s that she sailed again after rescue from what seemed a certain grave in the Caribbean. Despite an altered rig and deck that had disfigured the good looks of her youth, *Mariette*'s pedigree and speed potential were recognised by Tom Perkins. The walnut-panelled accommodation, remarkably still intact since 1915, was an added attraction.

OPPOSITE & RIGHT *Mariette* under full sail in a classic regatta. Many of her metal fittings, like the superb plate set into the end of her main boom, were cast in nickel aluminium bronze by Wessex Castings in England.

As *Mariette*'s new owner, Perkins embarked on a fantastic restoration programme. With a background in high-powered finance, he well understood the task at hand and did not shrink from the time and cost required to return the vessel to its original state, particularly the rig. Harry Spencer of Cowes in England was commissioned to build at least a dozen separate spars with all the standing and running rigging required for a topmast schooner capable of setting ten sails at once.

Wessex Castings in England made new nickel aluminium bronze deck fittings from drawings held at the Massachusetts Institute of Technology, where much of Nat Herreshoff's work was archived, and Ratsey & Lapthorn in the UK made a superb suite of hand-finished sails. All this was then shipped to the Beconcini yard in La Spezia, Italy, where it was fitted to *Mariette*'s steel hull. The interior was completely restored, and the full width saloon, with its remarkable walnut panelling, bookcases, glass cabinets, skylights and light fittings, remains one of the most outstanding examples of period yacht decor in existence.

It is her performance, though, of which *Mariette's* owner is most proud. Since her debut at the 1995 San Pellegrino Veteran Boat Rally in Porto Cervo, she has made a habit of winning on both sides of the Atlantic. On the race course, Tom Perkins is very much the skipper. He enjoys sailing her and is not afraid to pile on the 'canvas' when there's the prospect of a wild sail in the offing – a passion which Nat Herreshoff himself would surely have shared.

ABOVE LEFT & RIGHT The work which went into the deck houses, skylights and dorade (ventilation) boxes was extraordinary. Note the dove-tailed joints and detailing of the timberwork. The polished wood is solid teak.

OPPOSITE One of *Mariette*'s topsails lies along the teak laid deck. Setting this sail will involve sending at least one member of the crew aloft into the rigging to ensure it is in place. The crew member may also remain there while the yacht tacks. The sails were made at Ratsey & Lapthorn, the famous sailmakers of Cowes, England, who were making sails for large yachts in the last century and still do so today.

RIGHT & ABOVE A column of leathered hoops
connects the yacht's mainsail and foremain to their
respective wooden masts. They are seen here with the
sail in its stowed position, lying along the length
of the boom. Belaying pins are set around each mast
and are used for securing or belaying lines quickly.
As is traditional, the belaying pins are made of bronze.

RIGHT Well forward of the steering position is a comfortable seating area for al fresco dining or relaxing while the yacht is underway or at rest. The attention to detail that is apparent in the restoration of the yacht extends to the rich crimson upholstery with its embroidered cushions bearing *Mariette*'s name and silhouette.

BELOW *Mariette*'s fine spoked wheel set against the polished binnacle in which the steering compass is housed. The balls on either side of the binnacle are correctors which help to maintain the accuracy of the magnetic compass.

LEFT & BELOW LEFT & RIGHT The main saloon features extensive bookshelving, leather upholstery work and beautifully proportioned walnut panelling, which continues down the adjoining passageway. A period barometer and thermometer is one of a number of exquisite antiques aboard *Mariette*.

OVERLEAF There are few saloons which can compare with that aboard *Mariette*. Much of the interior detail is original and the saloon still retains an open fire. Note the fixing points for chairs to prevent them moving about while at sea. The panelling is walnut throughout.

ABOVE & RIGHT *Mariette*'s walnut-panelled dining saloon has all the old-world elegance and atmosphere of a London Club. During the day, natural light streams in through topside portholes to light the room, while in the evening it is illuminated by beautiful period light fittings and white candles in antique silver holders. As is customary on yachts of this calibre, *Mariette* is equipped with all her own crockery and silver cutlery.

ABOVE One of several comfortable and beautifully appointed single berths, this one is fitted with a leeboard (unseen) which keeps the occupant safely in position if the boat heels. Personal stowage lockers are situated outboard of the berth.

LEFT The owner's stateroom is panelled and painted cream. In keeping with the yachting tradition of the period, it is fitted with twin berths, with upholstered benches set either side of a polished chest of drawers. The huge skylight is opened using a winding mechanism and floods the room with natural light.

ABOVE The owner's private study, complete with period light fittings, leather-upholstered banquettes, and nautical artworks. Intricately carved timber retaining fiddles help to keep the books in place while travelling on the high seas.

OPPOSITE Even in classic yacht circles, the atmosphere and quality period finish found aboard Tom Perkins' *Mariette* of 1915 is considered superior. The painted walls of the study with their panelled trims echo the timber panelling of the passageway that leads to the yacht's magnificent, walnut-clad main saloon.

LEFT A bath was a rare luxury indeed for a yacht in the early years of the 20th century. But this one, and the period fittings which match, are much as they were when *Mariette* was built in 1915. In those days, with no water-making systems, filling a hot bath was a laborious process. Now hot water is simply piped through from a central, electrically heated tank.

BELOW The bathroom's original soap dish holder and towel rail – matching dolphins emerging from twin shells – are once again in full working order.

OPPOSITE *Linnet*'s simple yet efficient cockpit, with tiller steering and mainsheet arrangement aft. The wooden structure aft is the boom crutch which keeps the spar off the deck while at rest.

Linnet

New York 30

The yacht *Linnet* is a pristine example of a New York 30, designed by Nathanael Herreshoff for the New York Yacht Club in 1904 and now owned by Patrizio Bertelli, head of the Prada fashion house. Bertelli owns a number of classic yachts and has become one of the great yachting philanthropists of the late 20th century. When the simple little wooden gaffer, with her vast mainsail and purposeful bowsprit, was relaunched in 1997 after a complete restoration, she became the star of the classic fleets on the Italian and French rivieras. More importantly, perhaps, she now exists in near perfect condition as an example of Nat Herreshoff's superb eye for simplicity, efficiency and good looks.

She is typical of racing yachts of the early 20th century, built in a few weeks, using a basic but sound construction method. Although at the time expected by some critics to last no more than 20 years, many New York 30s outlived their original owners and a number were still racing in the 1980s. *Linnet* was built by the Herreshoff Manufacturing Company of Bristol, Rhode Island, for one Amos Tuck French. After numerous owners she was eventually found in the corner of a boatyard in Cape Cod, Massachusetts, by Federico Nardi, the owner of Cantiere Navale dell'Argentario in Porto Santo Stefano, Italy. He recognised a yacht that was well worth restoration and informed Patrizio Bertelli. *Linnet* was soon on a ship bound for Europe.

She is built of mahogany bottom planking and cyprus topside strakes on bent oak frames. Some of the mahogany had to be replaced, but most of the hull was in good condition, as were

OPPOSITE & RIGHT In almost every respect *Linnet* appears now as when she was launched in 1904. Her new mast, built by Cantiere Navale dell'Argentario, has simple rigging – the only hint of modernity is a wind instrument mounted high on the mast.

the wood keel, lead ballast and bronze keel bolts. Some of *Linnet*'s deck beams and the decks themselves were replaced, the latter with cedar strip. She is very much a day boat, typified by her numerous rectangular coachroof ports set into a simple, boxy coachroof trunking.

Most of the drawings for *Linnet* were available from the Massachusetts Institute of Technology's Hart Museum where many of Herreshoff's drawings are archived. Nardi and Bertelli were keen to return *Linnet*'s rig to as close to original as possible and new spars were made at the Italian yard. The only important omission in the reference was the length of the yacht's bowsprit. The New York 30s were designed with long or short versions. As *Linnet* was bound for the race course the longer version was chosen. Her new owner was keen to keep all her fittings as close as possible to the originals so checks were made against a New York 30 housed in the MIT Museum before any new casting moulds were made.

One of the really appealing aspects of *Linnet* is her simplicity, especially in her accommodation. Being so narrow (8ft 7in on a 30-ft waterline), space below is limited, particularly as the forward end of the coachroof trunking finishes abaft the mast. However, the simple berths, light-coloured upholstery, light soles, varnished deck beams and coachroof sides combine to produce a strikingly fresh and modern mood.

ABOVE & OPPOSITE *Linnet* was designed as a simple day sailer. When she was found by her current owner the decks were rotten and had to be replaced in authentic cedar strip and then painted as they would have been almost 100 years ago. Many of the deck fittings, like the bronze blocks, are either original or have been specially cast from drawings held at the Massachusetts Institute of Technology's Hart Museum. The cordage is made of modern plastics material fashioned to look like hemp.

OPPOSITE & BELOW Pure simplicity aboard *Linnet*. The tackle on the toerail is a runner assembly used to tension the rig and counteract the load of the headsail especially when sailing to windward. Runner tackles are also used to support the mast when sailing downwind. Other deck details – such as the boom crutch and mainsheet arrangement; square section bowsprit and sampson post; and curved coaming and coachroof – reveal Cantiere dell'Argentario's skill.

LEFT & ABOVE The starboard side sidedeck with wooden crutch about to be stowed. Yachts from the 1900s had no guard wires or stanchions, just small toe-rails. Characteristic of Linnet's classic simplicity is a beautifully varnished hatch with a glass prism set in its centre. This provides the accommodation below with an unusually generous amount of natural light.

RIGHT & BELOW The New York 30s were designed as day boats so accommodation is minimal. *Linnet*'s registration number and registered tonnage are carved into a beam running over her main bulkhead, the traditional location for such information. She is built of mahogany bottom planking with cyprus topsides (hull) strakes on bent oak frames. The yacht was not designed to last long but *Linnet* is a century old.

ABOVE Superb craftsmanship is evident in Linnet's streamlined accommodation. Rectangular ports built into the boxy coachroof sides allow an enormous amount of natural light into the saloon, making it appear bright and surprisingly modern.

RIGHT Although designed as a day boat, the accommodation is more than adequate, with settees in the main saloon and sleeping berths that can be used for overnight-ing. The white painted panelled bulkheads and deck heads, picked out with var-nished beams, posts and edgings, illustrate typical decor for the turn of the century.

Nº 201871

LEFT, ABOVE LEFT & RIGHT A minimalist head compartment that makes few concessions to modern times. Set into the polished timber bench is a metal basin operated by a hand-pumped water system. Details like this were recreated using Nat Herreshoff's original drawings.

OPPOSITE In her restoration *Linnet* does reveal some signs of the late 20th century. This modern lavatory in the head compartment is one. She is also fitted with an inboard engine. Originally she would have been engineless.

Orion

Topsail Schooner–147ft

Of all the restored yachts following the Mediterranean classic circuit, the 147-ft schooner *Orion* must be regarded as one of the most elegant. Designed by Charles E. Nicholson in 1909 for the King of Spain, she has a look about her few others possess – with a magnificent counter, extraordinarily deep bulwarks, sweeping sheer and deck houses. When her decks are fully lit at night, lying stern-to-the-dock in a favourite harbour like St Tropez, she stands out as something very special.

Although commissioned by the King of Spain, her first owner was one Courtney Morgan who named her *Sylvana*. She had a number of other owners before being sold in 1921 to the proprietor of the French newspaper *Le Matin*, when she was renamed *Pays de France*. It was her seventh owner, a Spaniard called Miguel de Pinillos from Cadiz, who called her *Orion*.

She passed through several hands before being laid up in La Spezia, Italy, where she started to deteriorate. Then, in 1978, her current owners started restoring her at the now defunct Valdettaro yard in Italy. *Orion*'s hull construction comprises mahogany planking on steel frames and considerable work has been done to maintain its integrity, including the removal of her copper sheathed bottom (fitted to protect against worm infestation). Her complex rig is now restored to original as a two-masted gaff schooner complete with separate topmasts.

It is to her owners' credit that instead of gutting her and building a new interior, they retained the yacht's extraordinary walnut panelled decor. An open fire with a brass fender,

OPPOSITE & RIGHT The Nicholson-designed topsail schooner under full fore and aft sail. Her rig, including her topmasts, was restored to its original state, transforming her performance and looks. She carries traditional lifebelts bearing her name.

a mantelpiece and candelabra, two large five-seater sofas, a writing table and a dining table for eight are all contained in a magnificent main saloon. At 23ft 6in wide, the saloon, like the owner's cabin, uses the full width of *Orion*'s hull, providing unusually spacious accommodation. A feature of the owners' cabin is a full-size bath.

Orion has walnut-lined cabins for ten guests, and there are berths for eleven crew forward of amidships. The yacht's galley resembles the kitchen of a turn-of-the-century Parisian restaurant. Carpets, light fittings, switches and skylights are all from the period in which she was built and together they create a powerful feeling of authenticity.

But behind all the panelling lies the paraphernalia of modern life. TVs, videos, hi-fi, CD, air-conditioning controls, drink coolers and cocktail cabinets are all in place, discreetly hidden away behind panelling until needed. As a charter yacht in both the Mediterranean and the Caribbean, such an inventory is a necessity.

Orion's owners have worked hard to maintain an aura more akin to that of the early 1900s when the yacht was first commissioned. This is unusual even in carefully restored classics. For this, judges in the 1999 circuit of classic regattas were quick to recognise the owners' achievement and rewarded them with prizes for technical authenticity. Although nearing her 100th birthday there seems little reason for *Orion* not to survive another century or more.

ABOVE & RIGHT Beautifully rendered details on deck include the ship's bell; specially cast bronze deck winches; elegant engine controls; and a skylight which provides natural light for one of many cabins below.

OPPOSITE The yacht's powerful mainsheet runs through a number of double or triple blocks to provide the purchase required to trim it in strong winds.

ABOVE LEFT & RIGHT *Orion* boasts a perfect example of a teak-laid deck. It is punctuated by deckhouses, hatches and neat rows of skylights which provide light and ventilation for the accommodation below.

RIGHT The schooner's elegant deck saloon remains much as it did when the yacht was launched in 1909. Designed by the famed Charles E. Nicholson for the King of Spain, the living quarters were intended to be suitably regal. The banister on the left leads down to the sleeping accommodation, galley and crew accommodation.

ABOVE The main saloon is designed to use the full beam of the yacht to create

accommodation with generous proportions. In this corner a writing desk, bookcase

and heavily upholstered settees create a particularly comfortable atmosphere.

OPPOSITE A polished staircase leads from the deck saloon down to the sleeping

cabins. Panelling throughout the yacht is in the distinctive yellow-brown tones of

walnut and many of *Orion*'s original fittings still remain.

ABOVE LEFT & RIGHT Handrail fittings are original, as is the fireplace in the main saloon which is capable of burning solid fuel. *Orion*'s owners have been careful to retain the yacht's period atmosphere by maintaining original fittings and resisting the temptation to replace them with modern equivalents.

LEFT *Orion*'s walnut panelled dining saloon provides a sumptuous atmosphere in which to entertain and easily accommodates an eight-seat dining table. The saloon is naturally lit by portholes set in the topsides and a superb skylight which can be opened using a screw driven mechanism (visible top right).

ABOVE, RIGHT & OPPOSITE Nowhere are the generous
dimensions of *Orion*'s living quarters more apparent
than in the bathroom adjoining the owners' cabin.
A full-size bath is a rarity in the bathroom of any
yacht of this size and period, not to mention the
quality of the fit-out. The timber panelling, shower
fittings, soap holders and towel rails are all original.

Partridge

Gaff Cutter—50ft

Some 20 years after he found her rotting on the east coast of England, Alex Laird has restored the 1885 gaff-rigged cutter *Partridge* to become the darling of the Mediterranean rivieras. His reward was victory on the race course and recognition by his peers of *Partridge*'s sympathetic restoration.

The cutter was lying waist-deep in mud when Laird stumbled upon her, but he spotted a yacht with a graceful line and, after paying just £200 for her, he set to work on his long labour of love. Considerable detective work was required to piece together the yacht's history. Eventually Laird discovered that she had been built by Camper & Nicholsons in 1885 and designed by J. Beavor Webb as a gentleman's day sailing yacht to be used for occasional racing.

Laird transported *Partridge* to the Isle of Wight where he spent seven years bringing her hull back to near its original state. Remarkably, for a yacht of her age, only five percent of the pitch pine planking had to be renewed, although most of her frames were irreparable. Undeterred, her dedicated owner bought 40 trees in Sussex from which he was able to fashion grown oak replacement frames. Other timbers were steamed and bent. He built a new deadwood out of laminated iroko and new deck beams were made out of oak bought in York. His training as a boat builder and naval architect was proving useful.

Partridge's survival could largely be attributed to her immense greenheart keelson, a 34-ft long piece of timber which forms the backbone of the yacht. After 114 years in position it was

OPPOSITE & RIGHT *Partridge* sails again after a 20-year refit. She has proved to be
particularly fast because she is relatively lightly built. Her restoration involved
making traditional fittings such as wooden blocks for the mainsheet arrangement.

still in perfect condition, its scalloped finish bearing evidence of the original
shipwright's adze. Also sound were the $1^1/_2$-in thick Burmese teak stringers,
which ran the whole length of the yacht. Progress was hindered, though, by
the fact that most drawings of *Partridge*, and those of similar yachts, had been
lost or destroyed. Lloyd's Register was able to produce some valuable construction details but Laird had to rely largely on photographs and his own
training as a naval architect to get things right. For instance, there was no reference for her gaff-rigged cutter sail plan nor for the dimensions of the spars.

In pursuit of just the right timbers, Laird travelled to Finland to buy
five trees which would eventually form the mast and other spars. Ideally he wanted Harry
Spencer, the famous Cowes-based spar builder, to do the work, but funds would not run to
this. However, Spencer supplied a shed which he extended, and encouraged Laird to do the
work himself. The 48-ft spar with a 30-ft topmast now carries all Harry Spencer's rigging and
a brand new suit of sails by the ubiquitous Ratsey & Lapthorn.

Laird's painstaking attention to detail has been rewarded since he relaunched *Partridge*
in May 1988. Not only has his prized yacht surprised many larger competitors with her turn
of speed at the Mediterranean regattas, but, perhaps more significantly, his restoration
work has been recognised by several judges for its authenticity.

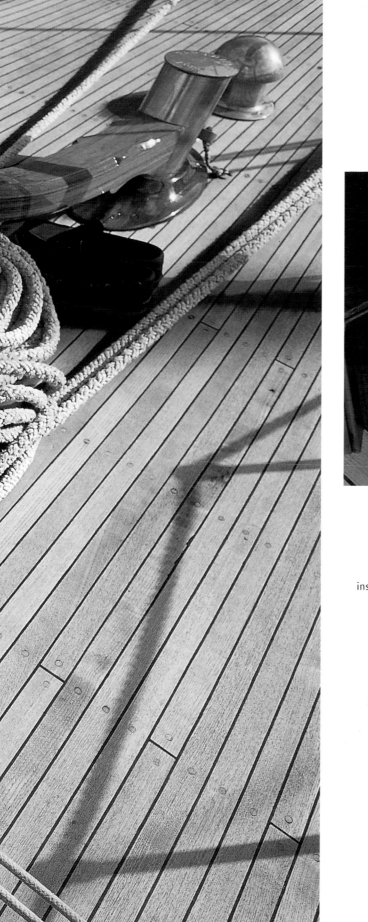

ABOVE One of the few concessions to modernity aboard *Partridge* was the installation of an inboard engine, a necessity for contemporary sailing. However, the controls, which are a period design, are discreetly hidden away so that nothing spoils the illusion of the yacht as it was when launched in 1885.

LEFT Magnificent detail surrounding *Partridge*'s elegantly shaped tiller. The brass binnacle on the left houses the steering compass which, for night sailing, is lit with an oil lamp set in the box attached to its side.

⚓

PREVIOUS PAGE The scrupulous attention paid by Alex Laird to period detail is visible everywhere on deck: in the ventilator cowling, the sheet tackle and sail cover and in the beautifully fashioned skylights and hatches.

RIGHT & BELOW *Partridge*'s forehatch leads down into her extensive, open plan accommodation. Her official number (ON) and registered tonnage (RT) are carved into the deck beam just below the main hatch.

⚓

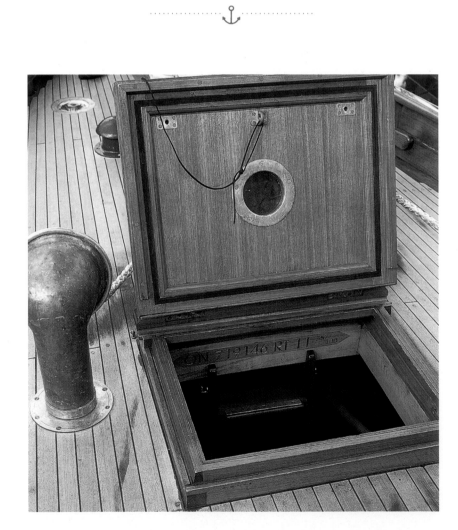

ABOVE After a day's racing, seaboots are left to dry wedged between the hull planking and the original Burmese teak stringers that run the yacht's length.

LEFT Despite the lack of furniture and the exposed frames, planking and stringers of *Partridge*'s hull construction, simple upholstered banquettes and plump cushions provide plenty of comfort.

The mighty *Creole*, launched in 1927.

Atlantide
Sailing Motor Yacht – 122ft

At first glance it would be easy to categorise *Atlantide* as a motor yacht. On closer inspection, though, it becomes clear that both her masts are capable of carrying sail and that her fore mast is equipped with a yard from which a squaresail can be set. *Atlantide* is owned and has been restored by Tom Perkins with the intention of using the 122-ft ship as 'supertender' to his classic schooner *Mariette* (acting as both a supply ship and luxury 'dormitory', especially when *Mariette* is racing). But being an avid yachtsman it was important to the owner of *Atlantide* that she should be capable of making way under sail as well as motor power. She is best described as a sailing motor yacht.

She was initially found in bad condition in Malta in 1998. Her attractive lines caught the eye of Tom Perkins, who discovered that she was an Alfred Mylne design originally built by Philip & Son of Dartmouth in 1930 for a yachtsman who wanted a tender for his yacht. It was a coincidence that appealed to him.

Atlantide was slipped in Malta, where the Manoel Island Shipyard undertook the complete re-plating of her steel hull. Only about a ton of the original steelwork now remains. The shell was then towed back to the UK where Camper & Nicholsons of Gosport started a year-long fit-out to a standard rarely seen in contemporary yacht building. To reduce weight aloft an aluminium deck was fabricated and then clad mostly in teak, successfully disguising any suggestion of the metal carcass that lay underneath.

OPPOSITE & RIGHT The laid decks aboard *Atlantide* are punctuated with specially made decklights designed to increase the amount of natural light below. *Atlantide* carries several launches including an unusual petrol driven example built in wood by Bugatti, the famous French car manufacturer, which also owned a small shipyard.

Tom Perkins returned to Harry Spencer of Cowes, who had worked on *Mariette*'s restoration, to build a new set of spars, Ratseys for the sails and Wessex Castings for the deck fittings. Both the 325-hp Gardner engines were lifted out and completely re-conditioned. For the accommodation Perkins commissioned Ken Freivokh's UK-based studio to design a complex Art Deco interior which would be constructed by C&C Designs of Norfolk, who had impressed with their work aboard Paul Getty's yacht *Talitha G*. The result was quite extraordinary.

The use of Lalique glass, mother-of-pearl and abalone inlays, madrona and macassar ebony marquetry, fibre optic edge lighting and specially engraved glass combined to produce a unique effect. Panel design inspired by the famous Art Deco work in the main lift of the Chrysler building in New York and a nymph motif discovered in the Paramount Theatre in Oakland, California, are examples of the detail developed by the Freivokh team.

Atlantide's extravagant interior makes her the perfect support boat for *Mariette,* based in Antibes in the south of France. Acres of teak-laid deck are available for après-race entertaining during the regattas held along the Italian and French rivieras, and guests can be accommodated in *Atlantide*'s immaculate cabins. And just in case of stormy weather, she is fully equipped with the latest stabilisers, ensuring guests can continue to enjoy smooth sailing.

PREVIOUS PAGE, ABOVE & RIGHT Fully restored by Camper & Nicholsons in Gosport, England, *Atlantide* flies the Maltese flag as Valletta is her port of registry. Her colours are picked out on her engine exhaust stack. Ventilators provide large amounts of air for the engine room where twin diesel engines are housed.

OPPOSITE *Atlantide* has been designed to act as a tender to the owner's classic racing yacht *Mariette* and provides a luxurious platform for entertaining, with seating for ten around her deck dining table.

ABOVE Exquisite detail can be seen in the ornaments and glasswork on the forward bulkhead in the main saloon. Considerable research was carried out to source artwork which inspired some of the designs set into the panelling. The gold-plated Art Deco style mask was designed and made by *Atlantide*'s owner.

LEFT *Atlantide*'s 1930s Art Deco interior is decorated with madrona and macassar ebony inlay marquetry and an abundance of Lalique glasswork. This is the main saloon which is edge-lit with a complex array of fibre optic fittings. The cigar box on the table is by Lalique.

ABOVE This unique skylight was designed by Tom Perkins, the enigmatic owner of *Atlantide*. Each glass prism is shaped in a certain way to provide an extraordinary explosion of light in the saloon below. The silicon bronze frame was hand built and each prism fitted at a precise angle to achieve the desired effect.

OPPOSITE The stairwell leading to the upper boat deck is protected by specially fashioned silicon aluminium bronze stanchions and rails. All the woodwork on deck is solid teak which covers a lightweight aluminium framework.

ABOVE Among the many works of art on board is this rare Lalique day and night clock set in a cabinet in the main passageway leading to the dining saloon.

RIGHT The dining saloon features a grand table setting, the centrepiece of which is a solid silver model of *Atlantide* made by the Langford Silver Vaults in the UK. The nymph sandblasted onto the glass bulkhead is based on a design from the women's lounge in the Oakland Paramount Theatre in the USA.

ABOVE The owner's sleeping cabin opens out into a small lobby which connects to the guest cabins and the stairwell leading to the main deck and the saloon. The portrait of Tom Perkins that hangs in the lobby is by his daughter.

OPPOSITE Ken Freivokh's inlay design for the panelling in the owner's cabin is clearly shown here. The white deckhead and hull lining offset the lacquered woodwork to great effect. Apart from the lacquer itself, this was a popular combination in yachts from the early and mid part of the 20th century.

ABOVE Decorated glass screens, marble bath and basin, ornate
tiling and plenty of light from the topsides ports make the
owner's bathroom particularly elegant.

LEFT A splendid double berth with massive bolsters dominates
the owner's cabin, which carries through the same Art Deco
design implemented by Ken Freivokh in other parts of the
yacht's accommodation. The central skylight provides
an excellent source of bright natural lighting.

ABOVE The owner's cabin is not the only one that has been beautifully furnished.
Atlantide boasts a number of VIP sleeping cabins which are luxuriously appointed.
Adorning one cabin is this magnificent Lalique *masque de femme*, a glass
panel taken from an original 1930s mould.

OPPOSITE Art Deco mirroring and dressing tables are among the furniture designed
especially for *Atlantide*'s VIP sleeping cabins. The silver shell cluster
displayed on the the table is an original Art Deco piece.

OPPOSITE A detail of *Tuiga*'s foredeck reveals the high quality of work undertaken by Fairlie Restorations during the complete rebuilding of the yacht.

Tuiga

15-Metre Class

William Fife of Scotland is regarded as one of the greatest naval architects of all time. Revered in sailing circles past and present, his reputation for producing the fastest, best looking yachts afloat is legendary. Some regard him more as an artist, unmatched in producing the ultimate sailing machines. No wonder then that yachts he was responsible for almost 100 years ago are now sought after by those hoping to restore a true classic. *Tuiga* is one such yacht and is an early example of a string of Fife designs, which are regularly sought out by Fairlie Restorations of Hamble on the south coast of England.

Duncan Walker, who runs Fairlie, had already gained a reputation for restoration following his work on the Fife schooner *Altair*. He found *Tuiga* in Cyprus, where she languished after years spent as a charter boat in the Mediterranean. Recognising her value, he bought her on behalf of a classic yacht philanthropist and towed her to Majorca. She almost sank en route but eventually arrived back in the UK where work began.

Tuiga was in fact commissioned in 1909 by the Duke of Medinacelli, a close friend of King Alphonse III of Spain, who was also a keen competitive sailor during the early years of the 1900s. *Tuiga* raced in regattas in the UK and Spain but, intriguingly, was rarely seen to beat King Alphonse's yacht *Hispania* in her home waters.

She is an example of a 15-Metre Class yacht, a type raced avidly by the British, Spanish and Germans at the beginning of the 20th century. Their massive, seemingly ungainly rigs

OPPOSITE Under full sail, *Tuiga* ghosts along in the Solent off the Isle of Wight, England, where in 1910 she and the other 15-Metre yachts regularly beat the local competition. The yachts were famous for their enormous mainsails and booms.

(the booms are 54ft long) and sail areas were due to T. C. Glen Coat, who published the 15-Metre rule in 1906. Despite their apparent ungainliness, the 15s enjoyed great racing. By the beginning of WWI, however, the rule was beginning to show its age, and when the new 12-Metre rule emerged the class all but died. It was not helped by the launch of *Istria*, a breakthrough 15-Metre with a new Marconi rig (so-called because the tall mast looked like the aerials used by the radio pioneer) which left existing 15s floundering in her wake. *Tuiga* had little opportunity for racing thereafter.

Duncan Walker's remarkable restoration of her in Hamble was meticulous. He used original drawings, enlarged Beken of Cowes photographs and other information from Archie Macmillan, the last general manager at Fife. The rig in particular was restored to original and even the decks, originally in pine rather than the harder wearing teak, are authentic.

She was re-commissioned in the spring of 1993 and soon returned to the Mediterranean, where the classic yacht restoration movement was gathering considerable momentum and organising late season regattas. *Tuiga* is now a familiar sight on the Riviera, her magnificent sail plan driving her at nine knots and more with the wind abaft the beam. When the wind is up she is capable of staying ahead of big schooners like *Mariette* and *Thendara*. She so impressed members of the Monaco Yacht Club, and in particular its commodore Prince Albert, that they bought *Tuiga* which now has pride of place outside the club in Monte Carlo.

ABOVE In a 15-Metre like *Tuiga* the skipper tends to sit on the boat rather than
in it when steering. Upwind, they are wet boats to sail but the coaming
does go some way to keeping the crew's seats dry.

RIGHT *Tuiga*'s kingplank, the piece of wood which runs down the centreline of
a yacht, and receives the ends of the planks that form the deck. In his meticulous
restoration, Duncan Walker laid the decks of the *Tuiga* using pine. Although not as
hard-wearing as teak, it was the timber originally used when the yacht was built.

LEFT *Tuiga* was unusual for her class in that she was built with particularly comfortable accommodation – perhaps the result of her owner's noble social standing. Her simple, elegant saloon features a dining table which doubles as a surface on which to lay out charts for passage planning.

BELOW The yacht's signal flags are stored in the centreline companionway. Once a means of communication, they are now used to dress *Tuiga* for regattas.

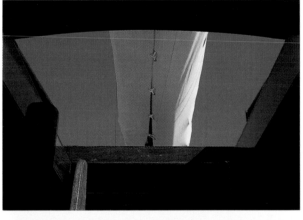

ABOVE Original fittings were maintained and
restored where possible and create a wonderful
period atmosphere aboard *Tuiga*.

RIGHT *Tuiga* may have been designed as a racing
yacht in the first decade of the 20th century but
there is no doubt that her first owner, the Duke of
Medinacelli, was intending to travel in comfort.
A gleaming galley adjoins the main saloon.

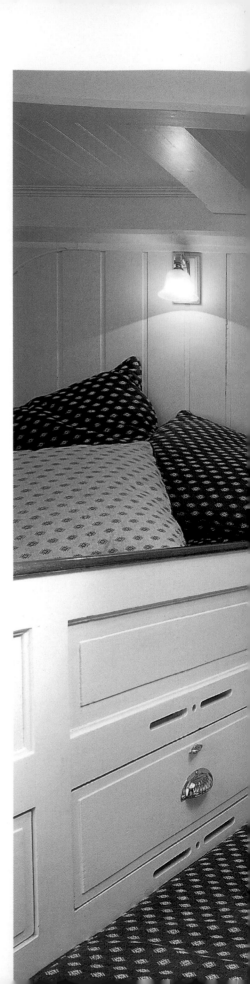

RIGHT & BELOW The layout of the sleeping
accommodation aboard is typical for yachts
of *Tuiga*'s era. Each cabin incorporates two single
berths set above chests of drawers, separated by
settees and a dressing table. The use of white painted
panelling throughout helps to reflect what limited
natural light there is entering the cabin.

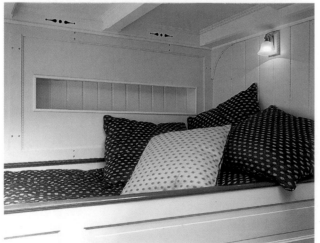

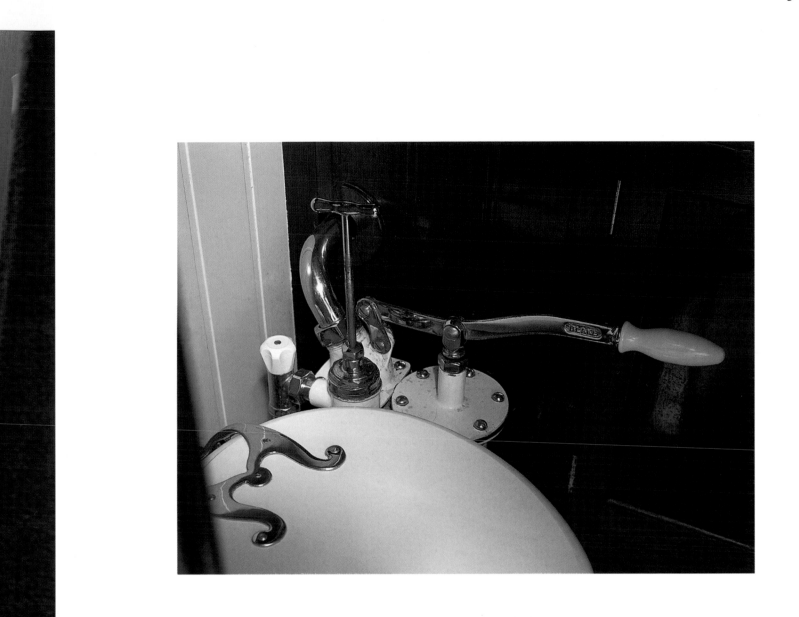

LEFT & ABOVE The authenticity of *Tuiga*'s restoration
extends to the bathroom or head compartment
(so-called because it was normally located at the head,
or forward in the vessel) where period shower
fittings and taps were either specified or restored.
The lavatory itself is a more recent model built
by Blake & Sons of Gosport, England.

Cerida

Bermudan Cutter–43ft

Jack Laurent Giles was one of the great English boat designers of the mid 20th century. Hallmarks of his distinctive style included pronounced bulwarks and deep cove lines which emphasised the shape of his yachts. These features were particularly apparent in Giles' design for *Cerida,* launched from Newman & Sons' yard in Poole, England, in 1938. She became so talked about in clubs and magazine articles that her building plans were donated to the Greenwich Maritime Museum in London.

Cerida was superbly built by Newmans using mahogany planking on oak frames with bronze fastenings and teak laid decks. Extensive hardwood hatches, skylights and companionways peppered her deck. Her length overall measured just 43ft but to look at her today she seems a much larger, more substantial sailing yacht. She was designed to displace just under 15 tons and with her long keel and sweet underwater lines she was guaranteed to give her passengers an easy ride in a seaway.

Over time, however, like so many yachts of her era, she has endured a string of owners who made alterations which undermined her authenticity. *Cerida*'s early years appeared to be unremarkable although it is known that she took part in a Fastnet Race in the early 1950s under the command of a member of the Royal Corinthian Yacht Club, participated in a number of classic yacht races and was also pressed into service in a sailing school. In 1955 she was sold to an Italian from Milan, one De Angeli Frua. She changed hands four more times, but

OPPOSITE & RIGHT *Cerida* sailing in her original trim in 1947. Her wooden mast was substituted for a metal version at one stage but thanks to her latest restoration now has a new wooden spar. Just as they might have appeared in 1938, the binnacle and compass are set into the kingplank with mainsheet blocks flanking it.

her home port was always Genoa and the Yacht Club Italiano. At some stage her deckhouse was enlarged and a skylight and an adjoining hatch were combined, presumably to create more space below. Her rig was shortened and replaced by an alloy spar, 3m shorter than the original and sporting a masthead sailplan. Alterations were also made to the owner's cabin and, on deck, the cockpit and tiller arrangement were altered.

She underwent a limited restoration programme at the Sangermani boatyard during this period and then in 1987 she was bought by Michele Amorosi, who lived aboard, chartered the yacht and maintained her himself.

After this litany of chop and change it seems extraordinary that anyone would want to take on a complete restoration, but for her present owner, Giuseppe Giordano, there was no doubt about *Cerida*'s potential. She was duly delivered to Cantiere Navale dell'Argentario where work began to bring everything back to original from truck to keel.

Strap floors, frames, hull planking, keel bolts, deck and all its fittings were inspected and restored, as were the interior and rig. A new wooden mast with a fractional sailplan with jumper struts was stepped and on 4 July 1999 she re-emerged almost as new. Since then she has gone on to claim honours in several regattas, and there seems little doubt that *Cerida* will now remain a small but bright star on the classic circuit in the Mediterranean.

ABOVE *Cerida*'s cockpit and deck layout are quite unusual in that the mainsheet and its winch are well forward of the steering position while the boom extends well aft over the head of the helmsman. The deep cockpit is the mark of a seaworthy yacht.

OPPOSITE The yachts designed by Jack Laurent Giles are almost unmistakable, characterised by their distinctive bulwarks, cove line and often a considerable amount of tumblehome (convexity) in the topsides aft.

ABOVE The restoration programme undertaken by
Cantiere Navale dell'Argentario included refurbish-
ment of the deck brightwork (varnished woodwork).

RIGHT *Cerida* has won enough trophies to make
any skipper proud, especially following her return
to the classic yacht circuit in 1999 and her
participation in the Prada Challenge series.

LEFT & ABOVE Despite enduring a string of owners who made unsympathetic alterations, *Cerida* has recaptured her former integrity, including the restoration of her hardwood hatches and skylight frames. One of her skylights opens up above the aft accommodation and chart table. The navigator has his own berth with instant access to the chart table and can communicate with the helmsman through the open skylight.

ABOVE A reading light illuminates the simple beauty of one of the yacht's four berths. Varnished beams and cappings with white painted panels, bulkheads and deckheads typify the finish for a yacht of *Cerida*'s era.

RIGHT The method of construction is revealed in the numerous deckbeams around the skylight of this cabin. The bunk would be fitted with a stout leecloth or even a leeboard when the yacht is heeled to starboard to keep the occupant securely in place.

OPPOSITE Deep bulwarks and a netting cradle provide some protection for the foredeck racing crew who have to work along *Moonbeam III*'s long bowsprit.

Moonbeam III
Gaff Cutter–102ft

The magnificent Edwardian racing yacht *Moonbeam III* was the subject of one of the most significant restorations of the late 20th century. Completed in 1979, it heralded a new and exciting era in the revival of classic yacht racing. So successful was her recreation that *Moonbeam III* is as active now as she was when she was first launched in 1903. Her rebuild is also considered significant for its authenticity.

Like many of the successful racing yachts of her time, *Moonbeam III* was designed by William Fife Jr and built by Fife & Sons of Fairlie in Scotland using teak and elm planking on oak frames. She measured 102ft overall and 81ft 5in on deck. She was commissioned by Charles Plumtree Johnson, whose father was then physician to Queen Victoria.

Moonbeam III stood apart from other yachts due to the outstanding quality of her accommodation and the way in which it was laid out. She then proved herself to be difficult to beat on the race course, a combination which resulted in a reputation second to none in the years before the outbreak of WWI.

After the war she was sold to M. F. Marconi, an industrialist from Paris, who originally moored her in Brest. There she won Le Coupe Antonide Julien before being moved to the Mediterranean. For the first time in her life, in 1924, she was fitted with auxiliary power, but the additional weight did not stop her winning La Course Croisière de la Mediterranée – one of the foremost competitions on the French Riviera. Her competitive days then looked to have

OPPOSITE & RIGHT Everything about *Moonbeam III*'s demeanour is redolent of the genteel Edwardian age, from her racing crew in their crisp white trousers and navy jerseys to the steering compass set in an elegant glass binnacle.

ended. She was bought by the pioneer aviator Felix Amiot and laid up in a shipyard in Cherbourg, where she remained virtually untouched for 23 years.

Moonbeam III's fourth owner was one Mme Anthony, who relaunched her in 1974. She took *Moonbeam III* to Greece where she was used as a charter yacht, and like many fine wood vessels deteriorated in the harsh Mediterranean conditions. But in 1979 her fifth owner shipped her back to England, where an immaculate restoration project began at Shamrock Quay under the direction of naval architect John Sharp. The hull was rebuilt, a new engine and generator installed and a navigation area added. A wheel replaced her tiller, but her vast gaff cutter sailplan was retained and improved. She now had all the facilities of a modern cruising yacht. Yet with her rich mahogany panelling – finished with silver and nickel-plated accessories – she retained her distinctive Edwardian character.

It was this sense of history that captivated *Moonbeam III*'s current owner, who bought the yacht after chartering her for part of a fascinating voyage taken in 1988. Under skipper and manager Philippe Le Chevalier, himself a one-time owner of the classic schooner *Lelantina*, she covered more than 15,000 miles. Starting in St Tropez she sailed to La Rochelle for the Whitbread Race stopover, then crossed the Channel to Cowes for the Hermès Mumm Trophy races before continuing on to Scotland to celebrate the Fife & Sons centenary – a dress rehearsal for her own 100-year birthday celebrations.

ABOVE Although she was designed as a racing
yacht, *Moonbeam III* is equally adept at providing
a comfortable platform on which to relax.
The table can be removed for sailing.

RIGHT *Moonbeam III*'s magnificent six-spoked wheel.
One concession to modern practicality and safety
was the installation of an engine – seen in evidence
here in the form of a control lever mounted
on the side of the steering mechanism box.

ABOVE LEFT & RIGHT A long stairway leads from the companionway to the yacht's spacious accommodation. The short, polished banister is wrapped with twine to provide a better grip.

RIGHT The control panel has been carefully designed so that the full-sized chart table and timber panelling do not conflict with the many modern systems required to make the management of a yacht like *Moonbeam III* viable today. Sailing instruments are mounted beneath the lockers.

LEFT & ABOVE The detailed restoration of
Moonbeam III has proved one of the most significant
projects in the recent development of the classic
yacht movement, due to the high quality of the work-
manship and the authenticity of the finished product,
both in evidence in the fully panelled dining area.
The design features – which include raised and fielded
interior panelling and elegant lighting sconces
– are typical of the Edwardian period.

ABOVE One of several comfortable Edwardian berths aboard *Moonbeam III*. As is typical of the era, the bunks here are set upon a substantial chest of drawers, and the inboard side of the hull is fully panelled for both insulation and decorative effect.

RIGHT & FAR RIGHT Edwardian bathroom fittings feature in the en suite facilities of this large twin cabin. Each bunk is set outboard of two upholstered settees.

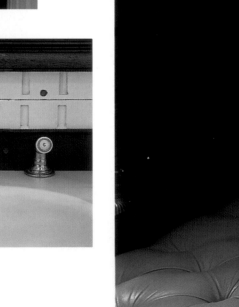

Cicely, **sailing in 1909.**

OPPOSITE Federico Nardi at Cantiere Navale dell'
Argentario has become legendary in restoration circles,
not least because of his achievement with *Dorade*.

Dorade

Yawl – 52ft

The contribution *Dorade* has made to ocean racing history is immense. That she still exists today in near perfect condition and continues to win races after some 70 years afloat is a tribute to her remarkable designer, Olin Stephens, and to those who have recently brought the yacht back to original condition. It is worth noting how well *Dorade* has stood the test of time. When she was launched she represented a breakthrough in ocean racing yacht design. Today she is regarded as a classic beauty, a perfectly balanced sailing yacht, still fast and able to undertake ocean passages in comfort. No racing yacht launched in the late 20th century will ever maintain that sort of appeal.

The 52-ft *Dorade* was commissioned by the American Roderick Stephens Sr as a way of encouraging his sons Olin and Roderick Jr, both naval architects. Olin was already working with Drake Sparkman, thereby establishing a partnership still unequalled in the history of small yacht naval architecture. Despite being just 21, Olin was able to draw on his experience designing 6-Metre and 8-Metre boats. Built by Minnefords, New York, in 1930, *Dorade* was at the time considered relatively small and lightly built, and was famously regarded as too fragile to race across the Atlantic. But this she did to great effect in 1932, finishing way ahead of her rivals both on handicap and on the water.

Through a change of ownership the yacht eventually made her way to the Pacific coast of America, where she won the Transpac Race in record time in 1936. After an active life on the

OPPOSITE & RIGHT In her original trim *Dorade* astounded the ocean racing world with a string of wins over much larger yachts. Much of her original detailing has been restored, including coachroof and winch plinths, and butterfly hatches and skylights.

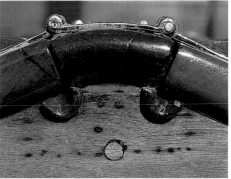

west coast she went up for sale in the mid 1990s. At that time she was based in Seattle, where although well used and raced she had not been maintained professionally. She was bought by the Italian Giuseppe Gazzoni Frascara and shipped to Federico Nardi's Cantiere Navale dell'Argentario. Her mahogany hull planking was replaced below the waterline; she was given teak decks to replace the existing cedar and plywood combination; and a new engine was installed almost amidships. The yacht was originally designed without an engine, so it was important to position the motor in a way that would least affect trim. Accommodating it required new, smaller steel frames and a hydraulic transmission system. Around all this the Cantiere constructed her exquisite accommodation joinery.

The wheel was discarded in favour of the original tiller arrangement, and her yawl rig is now very similar to that which existed in the 1930s. Her sails are cut in traditional, long panels, and lightweight Spectra halyards are used instead of wire, mainly to protect the varnished wood masts, but also to reduce weight aloft. As a result of these changes, *Dorade*'s success in the Mediterranean classic regattas now matches her all-conquering performances of the 1930s. In 1997 she won in Juan-les-Pins, Porto Santo Stefano, Palma, Porto Cervo and Cannes. The following year she was absent due to the loss of her rig while cruising, but that will undoubtedly prove to be a minor blip in this yacht's quite remarkable career.

RIGHT A walk around the deck of *Dorade* reveals many telling design features. Note the depth of the cockpit, the offset companionway and the ventilator cowls set upon dorade boxes – a new design which enabled air to enter the cabin but kept water out, and one of several pioneering nautical innovations found on board.

BELOW A closer look at the cockpit in post-racing mode. Most modern yachts of this size would be fitted with a wheel but *Dorade*'s long tiller is perfectly adequate aboard this immaculately balanced yacht.

LEFT & ABOVE The galley of *Dorade* was designed
for offshore racing circa 1930 – the U shape of the
work surfaces conveniently enables the cook to wedge
him- or herself in when seas are choppy. Positioning
next to the companionway also allows plenty of ventilation. The fiddles surrounding the surfaces keep items
in place while the yacht is heeled but the openings in
the corners allow for easy cleaning. While eminently
practical, the galley is also beautifully finished:
even the handpump is elegant and simple.

ABOVE, RIGHT & FAR RIGHT Cabins are comfortable yet streamlined. A foldaway sink in the head stows flat against the bulkhead when not required, but when in use drains into the lavatory bowl to save cutting another outlet in the hull. *Dorade* was considered lightly built but the vast 'hanging knees' which strengthen the deck-to-hull joint suggest otherwise.

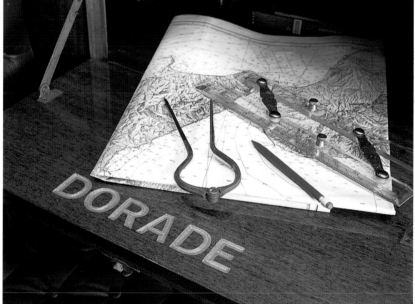

LEFT & ABOVE The wonderfully atmospheric main saloon is essentially masculine in feel, with little in the way of obvious decoration save for leather-upholstered banquettes and a framed photograph. One ingenious feature is a small foldaway chart table, which also doubles as a writing desk. There would be further provision elsewhere on the yacht for working on full-sized unfolded charts. Above the settee is a compact berth, known as a 'pilot' berth, which is used typically by the crew or off-watch for taking naps when passagemaking. This is actually the best place for sleeping as there is less motion here in the middle of the vessel.

Astra

23-Metre Class

The classic *Astra* was built as a 23-Metre Class yacht in 1928 for the sewing machine magnate Sir Mortimer Singer, as was the fashion for industrialists of the day. Designed by Charles E. Nicholson and built at the Camper & Nicholsons yard at Shamrock Quay, she was constructed of mahogany on metal frames with a yellow pine deck and cedar trim. At the time of her launch, *Astra* was considered particularly handsome. She also proved extraordinarily successful on the race course in her debut year. Her tally of five first places in the Big Class against yachts like *Britannia, White Heather, Lulworth, Shamrock* and *Cambria* was an outstanding record for a comparatively small vessel of 115ft and held the promise of great things to come.

Astra had started the season well, but tragedy overtook events when Sir Mortimer committed suicide in 1929 after a long bout of ill-health. Following his death *Astra* was retired from the racing arena. She was eventually bought by Hugh Paul – one-time owner of the Fife yawl *Sumurun* – and under his command the yacht achieved some even more remarkable results, not the least of which was winning the King's Cup three times.

In later years, she was relegated to cruising the Mediterranean under a cut-down rig but was eventually discarded. It was there that she was found in 1984, lying derelict on a beach in Salerno, by Italian Giancarlo Bussel. He bought the vessel and the process of her reincarnation began at the Beconcini yard at La Spezia. There much of her hull was rebuilt, while the 164-ft

OPPOSITE & RIGHT Although *Astra*'s alloy spars and many winches are not original, they do allow her to be sailed in relatively windy conditions. The ventilator cowls and butterfly skylights better reflect the era in which she was built.

spruce rig was replaced, and a phalanx of Lewmar winches were fitted to handle the lofty rig, giant sail plan and alloy spars. While not strictly authentic, the constraints of crew numbers in modern times made these changes essential.

She still retains her triple-headed cutter rig and in the right conditions is a very powerful sailing yacht. Perhaps the most noticeable change to her externally is the addition of a substantial deckhouse which alters her visual lines quite markedly from the original.

Below decks the style of the 1928 decor has been reproduced using oak panelling with a marquetry styling device throughout. One of the yacht's most extraordinary features is an oak-clad wooden bath which is set on the centreline between twin berths in the owner's suite. There is also an intriguing secret doorway leading from the owner's suite to one of the guest cabins. It is disguised as a built-in bookshelf, but at the press of a button it swings open to offer access to the adjoining quarters.

Shortly after her rebuild in Italy, *Astra* crossed the Atlantic and joined *Shamrock V* and *Endeavour* in a regatta at Newport, Rhode Island. It was an extraordinary event because the sail numbers K2, K3 and K4 came together for the first time in 50 years. In fact, *Astra* crossed the Atlantic several more times before returning to the Mediterraean, where she is now resident and very much part of the burgeoning classic fleet.

ABOVE A special feature of the deck saloon is a cabinet of cubby holes for stowing the signal flags – these days used for dressing the yacht rather than signalling other vessels, as in the era before radio communication.

RIGHT The large, comfortable deck saloon is panelled in polished oak and furnished simply with upholstered seats and plump colourful cushions. Guests can relax here – protected from the elements yet enjoying an excellent view of all the activities on board and beyond.

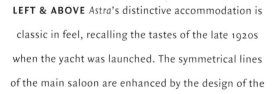

LEFT & ABOVE *Astra*'s distinctive accommodation is classic in feel, recalling the tastes of the late 1920s when the yacht was launched. The symmetrical lines of the main saloon are enhanced by the design of the oak cabinetry and panelling. Decorative devices include exquisite marquetry inlays and engraved-glass butterfly skylights which provide abundant light below.

ABOVE In the owner's cabin, a secret passage is disguised behind a built-in bookcase. At the press of a concealed button, the bookcase opens to reveal the passage leading to one of the guest cabins.

RIGHT Oak panelling is lighter in colour than the other hardwoods more often used for this purpose. The timber's pale gold tones create a brighter-than-usual atmosphere in the sleeping accommodation.

ABOVE Marble surfaces in the en suite bathroom facilities grace every guest cabin.
Some fittings are relatively modern compared with those which existed in 1928.

OPPOSITE Despite the fact that she was built as a racing yacht *Astra* was originally
fitted out to a very high standard, in keeping with her first owner's powerful position
as a captain of industry. Despite subsequent years of neglect the Beconcini yard
in Italy was responsible for bringing her back to this remarkable condition.
The passageway leading to the main saloon is evidence of her skilful restoration.

OPPOSITE The magnificent sweep of *Skagerrak*'s laid deck. Her counter bears a name which originated with a commission from the Kriegsmarine in 1939.

Skagerrak

Ketch–90ft

Launched on 8 August 1939, just before the outbreak of WWII, *Skagerrak* was commissioned personally by Grand Admiral Raeder for the Kriegsmarine, with the intention of using her for ocean racing and sail training for naval cadets. However, the Grand Admiral's plans were never to materialise, interrupted firstly by the war and finally scuppered at war's end when *Skagerrak* – like a number of other German sailing yachts – was claimed by the Allies and sailed to the United Kingdom. She spent at least 20 years there before being sold to her new owners, the Ranucci family, who commissioned the Beconcini yard to complete an extensive refit. She is now in excellent condition, with most features restored to original, and is based in Italy, where she enjoys a mixture of sedate cruising interspersed with some vigorous racing at classic regattas.

Skagerrak was originally built by the renowned Abeking & Rasmussen of Lemwerder, near Bremen, which has launched almost 6,500 private, naval and commercial vessels since Henry Rasmussen, a Dane, founded the yard in 1907. Rasmussen was an extremely keen yachtsman himself and his passion for seaworthiness and correct design was mirrored in the products that emerged from the north German yard. *Skagerrak* was no exception.

German sailing prowess had blossomed between the two wars and Abeking & Rasmussen were very much at the forefront of building large numbers of private yachts, both sail and power. *Skagerrak* would more than likely have been unleashed on the ocean racing scene

OPPOSITE & RIGHT Pictured under full plain sail, *Skagerrak*'s long, drawn-out counter and considerable sheer make for a good looking yacht. The 90-ft ketch was built by the Abeking & Rasmussen yard near Bremen in 1939.

to great effect. But with the German invasion of Poland in the autumn of 1939, German sailing activity was forced to come to an abrupt end. Construction of sailing yachts was abandoned as Abeking & Rasmussen's entire capacity was made available for the war effort. *Skagerrak*, described as a Hochseeyacht (offshore yacht), was one of very few of her type completed at that time. Most production in 1939 and the early 1940s was turned over to the construction of wooden mine sweepers.

Skagerrak measures almost 90ft in length overall and was originally rigged as a bermudan yawl with her staysail set on a jib boom. This arrangement has, in fact, been retained by the yacht's present owners. She was fitted with particularly large section wooden spars – no doubt in anticipation of some heavy work on the offshore race courses of Europe and America – and her mainmast towers 91ft 10in above the deck.

She was designed with a particularly attractive long, drawn-out counter, and with her fine overhanging bow she looks dependable and distinguished under full plain sail. On deck the skylights and deckhouses resemble the original designs quite closely and there is a distinctive steering position set up relatively high behind a protective screen, a useful facility while sailing in rough conditions. Her accommodation lacks the intricacy of many yachts of her era, perhaps a reflection of her intended career as a racing yacht and training vessel.

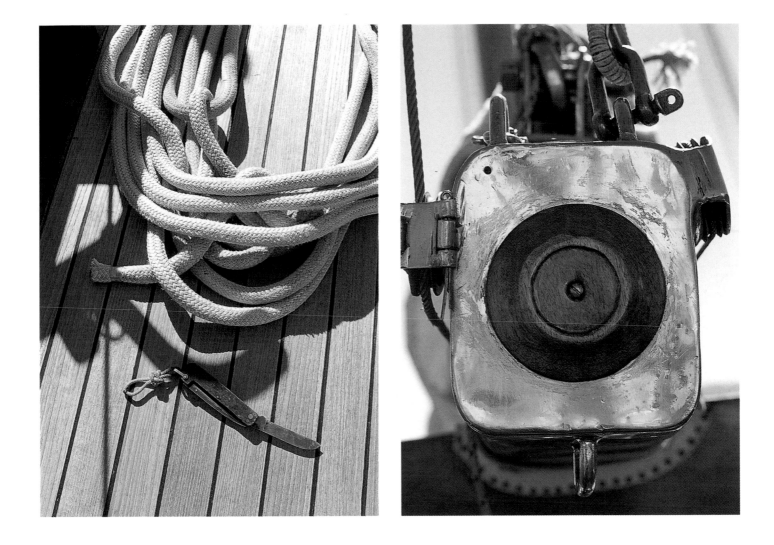

OPPOSITE, ABOVE LEFT & RIGHT The steering position provides an unusually generous amount of shelter – reflecting the needs of the Kriegsmarine which commissioned the yacht. Details on deck include coiled ropes and an intricately fashioned boom-end fitting incorporating various blocks and shackle eyes.

ABOVE & OPPOSITE As befits the disciplined lines of her exterior, functional

simplicity is the order of the day for *Skagerrak*'s interior fitout – as revealed here in

the main dining area and in the stairwell and passageways below decks. She is

impeccably maintained at the Italian yard of Beconcini where she spends her winters.

LEFT The modernist sensibilities of *Skagerrak*'s interior decoration extend through from the common areas to the accommodation. This stylish cabin with twin berths, set outboard, is divided by a dressing table and two bench settees. The treatment is less ornate than may be found on other classic yachts of the era – yet this functional approach typifies popular taste in Germany in the late 1930s.

BELOW Ornamental shell and coral displayed in one of *Skagerrak*'s guest cabins. Her owners have maintained the yacht's character and kept decoration to a minimum.

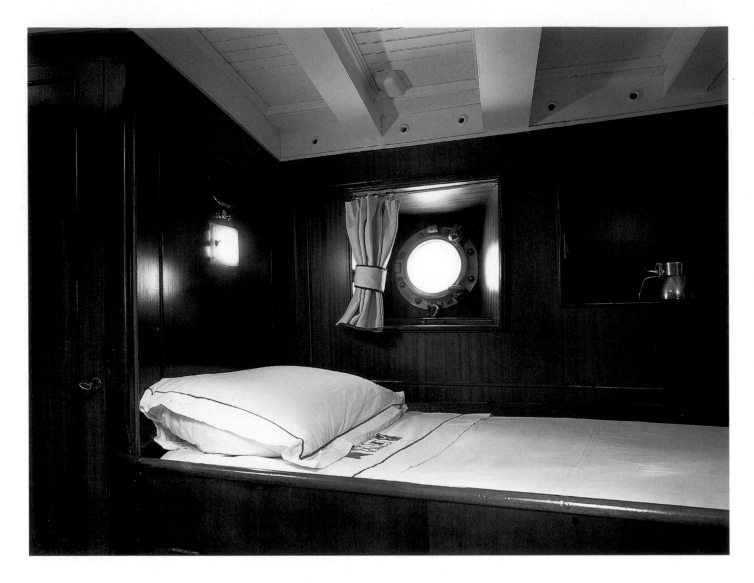

ABOVE A simple, single guest berth is provided with abundant natural and
artificial light. The massive deck beams and planked deckhead give the interior a
sense of security and solidity, but in fact are a result of the sturdy building required
for a yacht suited to northern European weather and waters.

OPPOSITE Pristine white towels in the en suite bathrooms are embroidered with
Skagerrak's profile and name. The porcelain sinks and plain fittings reflect the era in
which the yacht was built, when the modernist influence dominated German design.

180

OPPOSITE *Andromeda la Dea*'s automatic sail controls can be activated from the consoles forward of the wheel on the flying bridge deck. This area also serves as a place in which to relax when the yacht is sailing.

Andromeda la Dea

Automated Sailing Ketch–154ft

Andromeda la Dea was launched in 1990 and is typical of the highly successful class of yacht designed and built by Perini Navi of Viareggio, Italy, a pioneering force in automated yacht handling techniques. She was commissioned by Tom Perkins, an American venture capitalist who invented synthetic insulin and developed laser technology for industrial use. In less than 10 years Perkins has sailed *Andromeda la Dea* more than 100,000 miles. She has transitted the Panama canal twice and Suez canal once, rounded Cape Horn and cruised in Alaska. In 1999 she made the long haul from the Mediterranean to Auckland, New Zealand for the America's Cup final.

The luxury sailer incorporates many features which are synonymous with Perini Navi, in particular with founder Fabio Perini, who since 1983 has been a significant force in developing large, comfortable, long distance cruising yachts which can be sailed short-handed, allowing just two or three people to do the work of fifteen. This is in large part thanks to Perini's re-invention of the ubiquitous sheet winch.

On a yacht like *Andromeda la Dea*, measuring 154ft and weighing more than 340 tons, conventional winches operated by hand are too small and dangerous to use. Instead, Perini designed and built the captive or reel winch, an electro-hydraulically driven drum which automatically takes in or eases the sheets which control each sail. The winches are operated remotely from the yacht's steering position and are equipped with a safety device which auto-

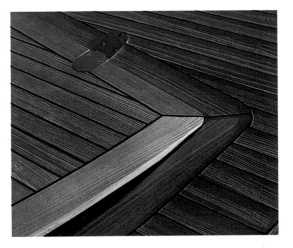

OPPOSITE & RIGHT Perini Navi, the Viareggio-based yacht builders responsible for *Andromeda la Dea*, built everything from the complex aluminium masts to the perfectly fashioned teak-laid decks. Hatch covers are also skinned in teak to match the deck.

matically releases the sheet if the loading upon it becomes too great. The captive winch can be hidden in an underdeck locker thus keeping the decks clear of unsightly equipment. It also means that heavily loaded and potentially dangerous sheets can be run beneath the decks, out of harm's way. Other innovative features include a hydraulically-lifting, fully-ballasted centreboard weighing more than 20 tons which allows the yacht to visit anchorages which would be inaccessible with a deeper, fixed keel. She draws 23ft with the keel down and 11ft with it up.

Tom Perkins worked closely with Fabio Perini in the development of his yacht. One result of this was the unusual transverse track at the top of the yacht's mizzen mast. Keen to realise all *Andromeda la Dea*'s potential, Tom Perkins felt that the trim of the fisherman, the sail which sets between the two masts, could be improved, so he suggested a track which enabled the sheet lead to be varied. The system worked and is now almost standard on Perinis.

Another unusual aspect of the Perini philosophy is that the accommodation layout within the steel hulls is almost standard. The yachts are often built on a speculative basis so that clients can, in effect, buy them off the shelf, dramatically reducing delivery time. Yet there is nothing formulaic about Tom Perkins' yacht. A mood of understated luxury pervades, with polished teak panelling throughout, distinctive buffalo hide upholstery, a working fireplace in the main saloon and an abundance of natural light in both living and sleeping quarters.

ABOVE Guard wires make *Andromeda la Dea*'s side decks secure; the flying bridge
is fitted with a series of instruments which provide wind direction, speed and angle;
the superstructure is built in lightweight aluminium and finished with aircraft
quality paint systems – the teak deck itself is bonded onto the metal surface.

OPPOSITE *Andromeda la Dea* is one of the most interesting contemporary yachts
to have emerged from the Perini yard, which itself has been responsible
for a revolution in automatic sailing.

ABOVE LEFT & RIGHT The Perini Navi logo adorns the superstructure of all 24 yachts the company has built since 1986. *Andromeda la Dea*'s custom-built, removable boarding ladder is suspended from the yacht's toerail, but can be removed and stowed when the vessel is underway.

OPPOSITE Form meets function aboard *Andromeda la Dea*, whether in the sophisticated controls on the yacht's flying bridge or the dynamic spiral stairway which descends from the flying bridge to the main deck.

ABOVE & OPPOSITE The leather upholstered furniture in the main saloon is

specified as standard by Perini. Customers can choose their own colour schemes. The

natural lighting is supplemented with halogen deckhead lights and a centrelight

with diffused glass shades. There is still plenty of scope for personal touches, such as

the half model of *Andromeda la Dea* which adorns one of the panelled bulkheads.

LEFT & ABOVE Centrepiece of the main saloon is a
working open fireplace which makes the seating area
in this area of the yacht a comfortable place to read
and relax (in hot weather, there is air conditioning
throughout). Above the mantelpiece hangs a painting
of racing schooners. The starboard-side passageway
leads from the main saloon through to a bar and
Andromeda le Dea's extensive dining area.

RIGHT Surrounded by the warm tones of teak panelling and rose pink upholstery, guests can relax in the bar area, which adjoins a large dining area. A staircase descends to give access to the expansive owner's suite, sleeping accommodation for six guests in three cabins, and the engine compartment.

BELOW An antique model ship is set in a glass case located in the passageway between the main saloon area and the dining saloon. Artwork is either fixed in position or moved to custom-built stowage lockers when the vessel is at sea.

⚓

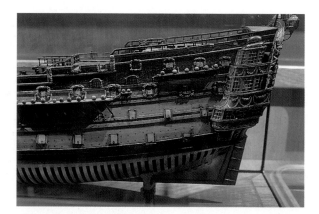

LEFT & ABOVE The owner's suite, which includes a private study, sleeping accommodation and bathrooms, is situated below the main deck. This area of the yacht is exceptionally quiet – cabins and furniture 'float' on rubber shock absorbers to improve sound insulation and to reduce vibration from the machinery room situated in the stern. The study is equipped with sailing instrument read-outs.

RIGHT & BELOW The owner's sleeping cabin is illuminated with natural light which streams in through topsides portholes. The sole of this cabin is just below the waterline. By using *Andromeda la Dea*'s entire 30ft 2in beam in their design for the accommodation, Perini has allowed plenty of space for sofas and tables. The sextant in its case on the coffee table is not just intended for display. In addition to modern navigation aids, yachts still carry a sextant for position-finding in the event of a satellite system shutdown.

⚓

OPPOSITE *Tiketitan*'s specially moulded mainsail is automatically stowed by furling it around a mandrel set within the main boom, the shell of which is carbon fibre. Sails can be trimmed at the press of a button.

Tiketitan

Canting-Keeled Sloop—88ft

During the 1990s, the Monaco-based Wally Yachts organisation engineered a revolution in the design of large, high performance sailing yachts. Behind this movement was Luca Bassani, an accomplished racing yachtsman whose inventive mind led to a string of unusual designs, the most extreme being *Tiketitan*.

With her hull designed by the celebrated Argentinian naval architect German Frers, Bassani's own team then filled the ultra light *Tiketitan* (the 88ft 7in yacht weighs just 29tons) with innovative features, the most remarkable being a 12ft 5in keel which cants from side to side to improve performance. The canting keel had been restricted to use on racing yachts, but for the first time a performance cruising yacht was benefitting.

Bassani was not only interested in a yacht which would be fast in the Mediterranean's generally light weather conditions. He wanted a yacht which was stylish and extremely comfortable to live aboard, a day racer with luxury accommodation. To keep weight to a minimum *Tiketitan*'s furniture is made of a material used in the aerospace industry – a lightweight 'honeycomb' cored veneer. Although it looks like solid wood it is a fraction of the weight.

Another important requirement was being able to handle *Tiketitan* with just two crew. Beneath the cockpit coamings lie large electro-hydraulic, automatic winches, operated from the steering position by the touch of a button. *Tiketitan*'s moulded plastic sails are rolled onto furling devices which are driven by electric motors – all 4,000 square feet of sail can be set in less

OPPOSITE & RIGHT The view from the top of *Tiketitan*'s towering mast clearly shows the large stern platform leading to the accommodation. When sailing, the yacht's keel can be canted to reduce the angle of heel and thus sail faster.

than five minutes. A century ago it would have taken ten men half an hour to do the same job. The jib is self-tacking so when the yacht is put about there is no need to let go or take in ropes. Half a turn of the steering wheel is all that is needed to set off on a new tack.

Tiketitan has raised a few eyebrows in the Mediterranean, where raw speed is normally the preserve of the so-called maxi class fleet and specialist grand prix racing boats. The skilful Bassani and his hi-tech flier regularly beat much larger yachts, and yet when *Tiketitan* is moored to the dock in St Tropez or Porto Cervo her owner can relax in sumptuous accommodation.

Being a yacht intended primarily for the Mediterranean climate, special provision has been made for al fresco living. Instead of a conventional afterdeck, 15ft or so of *Tiketitan*'s hull has been 'scooped out' to leave a vast stern platform. The level of the deck here is just a few inches above the waterline, creating a fantastic sensation of speed when sailing. When the yacht is moored stern-to, Mediterranean style, guests can simply step aboard rather than having to clamber up a long pasarelle.

It would be wrong to categorise *Tiketitan* as simply a gimmick. Ahead of her time she may indeed be, but she is certainly one pointer to the way in which most people may go sailing in future – whether competitively or for pure relaxation.

ABOVE LEFT & RIGHT Stylish design and branding characterises *Tiketitan* throughout. Cockpit speakers provide concert quality reproduction on deck. The open stern
is dramatically exciting at sea and practical while moored stern-to. A satellite
communications dome is mounted on the titanium rail.

OPPOSITE Carbon fibre is not only used in the construction of the hull and internal
structures; it is also integral to the interior design. Here it is used for the sole, or
floor, of the yacht's accommodation, contrasting with the timber of the furnishings.

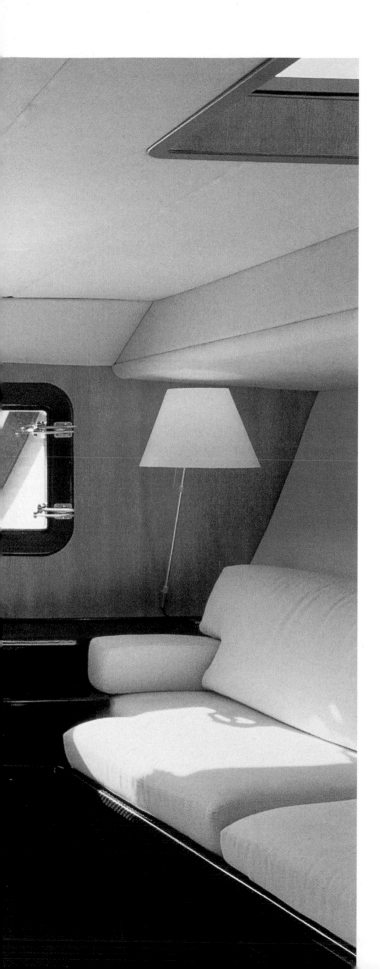

ABOVE A detail of the companionway stairs, which lead from the main saloon to the yacht's large stern platform. To save weight the woodwork is formed of an extremely thin wood veneer bonded to an ultra lightweight honeycomb core.

LEFT The saloon is dominated by a dining table which is suspended on a carbon fibre cantilevered arch.

OPPOSITE The Wally team's trademark clean lines and minimalist, streamlined design are apparent in this high-speed waterborne apartment.

RIGHT & BELOW Although *Tiketitan* is designed as a high-speed sailing yacht with revolutionary handling systems, the provision of comfortable accommodation for owner and guests is also important. Each sleeping cabin has its own en suite shower and toilet compartment, finished in a pale wood veneer.

NAUTICAL GUIDE

SHIPYARDS

Abeking & Rasmussen
An der Fähre 2
D-27809 Lemwerder
Germany
tel: 49 421 67330

Alloy Yachts International Ltd.
1 Selwood Road, Henderson
Auckland, NZ
tel: 64 9 838 7350

Camper & Nicholsons
Mumby Road, Gosport
Hants PO12 1AH, UK
tel: 44 2392 580 221

Cantiere Navale Beconcini
Viale S. Bartolomeo 428
19138 La Spezia, Italy
tel: 39 0187 524 127

Cantiere Navale dell' Argentario
Loc. Valli, 58019
Porto S. Stefano, Italy
tel: 39 0564 814 115

Fairlie Restorations
Unit 17, Port Hamble,
Satchell Lane, Hamble
SO31 4NN, UK
tel: 44 2380 456 336

Feadship
PO Box 70
2110 AB Aerdenhout,
The Netherlands
tel: 31 23 524 7000

Hinckley Company
PO Box 699
Southwest Harbor
ME 04679, USA
tel: 1 207 244 5531

Intermarine Yachting USA
301 North Lathrop Avenue
Savannah, GA 31415
USA
tel: 1 954 764 4600

Nautor
PO Box 10
FIN 68601, Pietarsaari
Finland
tel: 3586 760 1111

Palmer Johnson Inc.
PO Box 109
61 Michigan Street
Sturgeon Bay, WI 54235
USA
tel: 1 920 743 4412

Perini Navi SpA
Via M. Coppino 114
55049 Viareggio
Italy
tel: 39 0584 4241

Vitters
Stouweweg 33
8064 PD Zwartsluis
The Netherlands
tel: 31 38 386 7145

Wally Yachts
8 Avenue des Ligures
98000 Monte Carlo
tel: 377 93 100 093

DESIGNERS

Alden Inc., John G.
89 Commercial Wharf
Boston, MA 02110
USA
tel: 1 617 227 9480

Jon Bannenberg
6 Burnsall Street
London SW3 3ST, UK
tel: 44 207 352 4851

Philippe Briand Yacht Architecture
41 Av. Marillac,
1700 La Rochelle
France
tel: 33 546 505 744

Alan Buchanan Naval Architect
La Ville au Bas,
St Lawrence, Jersey
Channel Islands, UK
tel: 44 153 486 5536

de Voogt International Ship Design & Engineering
PO Box 70
2110 AB Aerdenhout,
The Netherlands
tel: 31 23 524 7000

Terence Disdale Design
31 The Green
Richmond, Surrey
TW9 1QQ, UK
tel: 44 208 940 1452

Dubois Naval Architects & Yacht Design
Beck Farm, Sowley Lymington
Hants, SO41 5SR, UK
tel: 44 1590 626 666

Farr & Associates
613 Third Street, Suite 20
Annapolis, MD 21403-0964
USA
tel: 1 410 267 0780

Ken Freivokh Design
Ash Studio
Crocker Hill Fareham
Hants PO17 5DP, UK
tel: 44 1329 832 514

Frers Yacht Design
Guido 1926, 1er piso
Buenos Aires 1119
Argentina
tel: 54 11 4806 4806

Laurent Giles Naval Architects
The Station
Lymington
Hants, SO41 9AZ
tel: 44 159 067 3223

The Hinckley Company
130 Shore Road
Southwest Harbor
ME 04679, USA
tel: 1 207 244 5531

Hoek Design Naval Architects
Grote Kerkstraat 23
1135 BC Edam
The Netherlands
tel: 31 299 372853

Ron Holland Design
28 Lower O'Connell
Kinsale
County Cork, Ireland
tel: 353 21 774 866

Bruce King Yacht Design
Newcastle Square
PO Box 599
Newcastle, ME 04553
USA
tel: 1 207 563 1186

Ollier & Associates
Le Parc du Golfe
Vannes 56000
France
tel: 33 297 409 844

Paola Smith & Associates
300 Northeast 3rd Avenue
Suite 150, Ft Lauderdale
FL 33316, USA
tel: 1 954 761 1997

Pedrick Yacht Design
Three Ann Street
Newport, RI 02840
USA
tel: 1 401 846 8481

Sparkman & Stephens
529 Fifth Avenue, 14th fl.
New York, NY 10017
USA
tel: 1 212 661 6170

Luigi Sturchio & Partners
Via Castelguidone 4
00159 Rome, Italy
tel: 39 064 384 462

Redman Whitely Design
33 Chelsea Wharf
15 Lots Road
London SW10 OQJ, UK
tel: 44 207 349 0240

CHARTERS

Ardell Yacht & Ship Brokers
PO Box 2328
Newport Beach
CA 92659
USA
tel: 1 949 642 5735

Balstram & Brakenhoff
2 Marina Plaza, Goat Island
Newport, RI 02840
USA
tel: 1 401 846 7355

Bounty International
1535 Southeast 17th Street
Suite 119, Ft Lauderdale
FL 33316, USA
tel: 1 954 524 9005

Luke Brown & Associates
1500 Cordova Road
Suite 200, Ft Lauderdale
FL 33316, USA
tel: 1 954 525 6617

Nigel Burgess
The Monte Carlo Sun
74 Blvd. d'Italie
98000 Monaco
tel: 377 93 502 264

Camper & Nicholsons
25 Bruton Street
London W1X 7DB, UK
tel: 44 207 491 2950

Castlemain Yachts Inc.
PMB 780
757 Southeast 17th Street
Fort Lauderdale, FL 33316
USA
tel: 1 954 760 4730

Cavendish White Ltd
4 Bramber Court
London W14 9PW, UK
tel: 44 207 381 7600

Crestar Yacht Charters
125 Sloane Street
London SW1X 9AU, UK
tel: 44 207 730 9962

Edmiston & Co.
51 Charles Street
London W1X 7PA, UK
tel: 44 207 495 5151

Fraser Yachts Worldwide
2230 Southeast 17th Street
Ft Lauderdale, FL 33316
USA
tel: 1 954 463 0640

Hinckley Crewed Charter
PO Box 6
Southwest Harbor, ME 04679
USA
tel: 1 207 244 0122

Peter Insull's Yacht Marketing
19 Av du 11 Novembre
06600 Antibes
France
tel: 33 493 34 22 42

J-Class Management
28 Church Street, Newport
RI 02840, USA
tel: 1 401 849 3060

Lynn Jachney Charters
PO Box 302, Marblehead
MA 01945, USA
tel: 1 781 639 0787

Moncada di Paternó Ship & Yacht Brokers
Via Montenapoleone 8
2021 Milan, Italy
tel: 39 02 7600 4649

Nautor's Swan Charters
Coddington Wharf
15 Goodwin Street, Newport
RI 02480, USA
tel: 1 401 848 7181

Nicholson's Yacht Charters
29 Shirman Street
Cambridge, MA 02138
USA
tel: 1 617 661 0555

Northrop & Johnson
0 Lee's Wharf
Newport, RI 02840
USA
tel: 1 401 848 5540

Offer & Associates International
2945 State Road 84
Suite A1, Ft Lauderdale
FL 33312, USA
tel: 1 954 587 0935

Rex Yacht Sales
2152 Southeast 17th Street
Suite 202, Ft Lauderdale
FL 33316, USA
tel: 1 954 463 8810

Bob Saxon Associates Inc.
1500 Cordova Road
Suite 314, Ft Lauderdale
FL 33316, USA
tel: 1 954 760 5801

Merle Wood & Associates
888 East Las Olas Blvd., 3rd fl.
Ft Lauderdale
FL 33301, USA
tel: 1 954 525 5111

Yachting Partners International
28-29 Richmond Place
Brighton
Sussex BN2 2NA, UK
tel: 44 127 357 1722

SPECIALIST SUPPLIERS

Captain Watts
7 Dover Street
London W1X 3PJ, UK
tel: 44 207 493 4633
London chandlery and mail order

Newport Yacht Services
PO Box 149, Newport
RI 02840, USA
tel: 1 401 846 7720
complete service for superyachts

Raffles Marina
10 Tuas West Drive
Singapore
tel: 65 861 9000
leading chandlers in southeast Asia

Ratsey & Lapthorn
42 Medina Road, Cowes
Isle of Wight, PO31 7BY, UK
tel: 44 1983 294 051
makers of traditional sails

Simpson Lawrence.
218-228 Edmiston Drive
Glasgow G51 2YT, Scotland
tel: 44 141 427 5331
global supplier of all chandlery items

Spencer Rigging
St. Mary's Road
Cowes, Isle of Wight, UK
tel: 44 1983 292 022
specialist mast builders and riggers

INDEX

ACKNOWLEDGMENTS

The publishers thank all those who graciously allowed their yachts to be photographed, and to the managers and captains for their kind cooperation. For their invaluable assistance the author and publishers also gratefully thank: Gianni Loffredo, Luigi Lang, Carlo Pasanisi, Tom Perkins, Federico Nardi, Valeria Palombo, Michael Horsley and Pascale Moll of Malcolm J. Horsley, Dr. William Collier, Monica Paolazzi and Monica Merani at Wally Yachts, Elizabeth Meyer and Marcia Whitney at J-Class Management, Maguelonna Turcat, Captain Paul Goss, Jeff D'Etiveaud, Peter Stone, Valeria Palombo, Silvia Frediani at Perini Navi, James Hatcher at Pendennis Shipyard, Justin Redman at Redman Whiteley Design, Myriam Marazzini at Vega Shipping, Rosemary Hamilton, Greg Powlesland, Lisa Vincenzini, Gwynn-fyl Lowe.

Additional photographs courtesy of: Mary Evans Picture Library 2, 208. Beken of Cowes 4-5, 7, 8, 11, 12 ,13, 18, 41, 56, 70, 80-81, 86-87, 104, 118, 130, 140-141, 144, 156, 168, 178-179. Perini Navi (ph. Bob Grieser) 182. Wally Yachts back cover tr, 198-207.